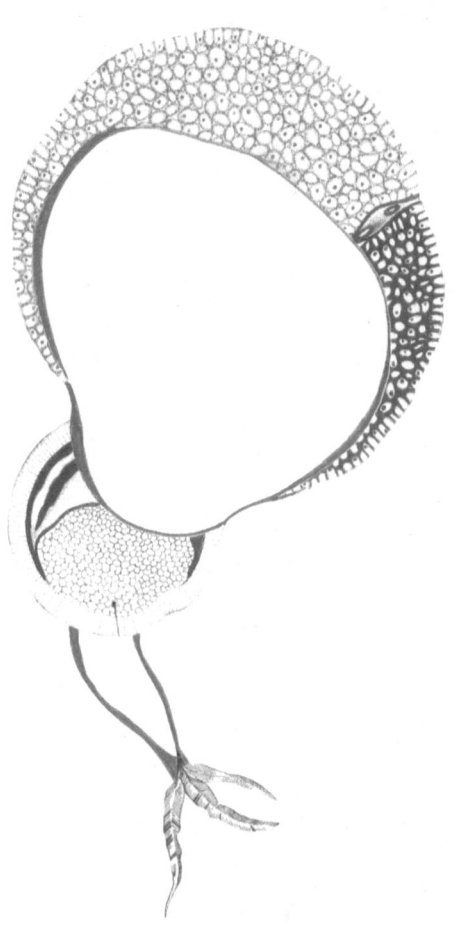

CENTIPEDE

POEMS BY

SASHA GOODWIN

Maine Chapbook Series
Maine Writers & Publishers Alliance
2023

For Joe Millar who taught me to see language anew and Amy Schrader for decades of editing and patient friendship.

ISBN: 978-1-7356732-6-4

©2023
Published in the United States of America
by the Maine Writers & Publishers Alliance
Portland, Maine

Publication made possible by grants from the Maine Arts Commission, the
Margaret E. Burnham Charitable Trust, and the Nichols Fund.

Cover & interior images by Elizabeth Snowdon
Author Photo by Sasha Goodwin

Published in collaboration with Pink Eraser Press.

CONTENTS

Introduction

Predictable 13
Suitcase 14
Let's Not Pretend 15
Block Captain 16
Sometimes 17
Brine 18
In Your Absence 19
Dry Land 20
Poem about the Night 22
Seattle, 2019 23
We Talk 24
Birches 25
Genius 26
Matchbox 27
Tire Swing 28
Untitled 29
Losing 30
Chicken Basket 32
Letter to the Owner of an Old Wool Suit 33

INTRODUCTION

It is rather fitting, I think, that *Centipede* is a collection of poems which takes its title from a small creature known and named for its many legs; this is a book with all manner of instruments on display, each of which contributes to its elegant forward propulsion. The text is a bestiary filled with creatures both tame and untamed: all of them roaming unfettered, unabashed, totally free.

At the level of both content and elaboration, it is unlike anything I have read in recent memory. There are echoes, to be sure, of various poets from throughout the 20th and 21st centuries—Alfred Starr Hamilton and A.R. Ammons, to name a pair—but the arrangement of the materials offered by these and other mystics throughout the American tradition feels new, and alive. The collection transports you elsewhere. It transforms you. At every turn, it brings us back to both "beauty and decay," reminds us that they are "always passengers on the same train."

And so, we must study loveliness and destruction, alienation and intimacy, terror and ineradicable joy. One gets the sense that we are being guided through a world on the cusp of great transformation, an arrangement in which we can no longer ignore the ways we are bound to the plants and animals, ancient and otherwise—the wooly mammoths and African grey parrots and ferns and thawing maples and prairie dogs—with whom we share the planet.

Centipede asks us to expand our vision, re-orient our looking. To lose ourselves in the blur between the untamable outside world, and the sense of transcendent possibility that we carry within.

—Joshua Bennett, 2022 Maine Chapbook Series Judge

CENTIPEDE

PREDICTABLE

Spring bent the wire feet
of birds around each thin branch
along Denny Avenue. A splendid screech
of tires on wet pavement
announces the resurrection of Christ
who is a blue kite against a cloudless sky
taking inventory: hobos airing their feet,
firemen touring a charred house,
and a tiger moth's wings
like veined flames in a child's drawing.
I am startled by spheres of white blooms.
My conception of symmetry just out of reach
and then behind me as I trace the perimeter
of the park. Ducks collide above the reflecting pool
and scold one another. A cacophony of conversations,
strangers' faces, and air outlining the trees.
This vivarium reflected in the faceted eye
of a regal horsefly, stonemyia tranquilla.
Once the birds pair up their songs cease
and then the nestlings.

SUITCASE

Inside a music box we see
a real African Grey. Each object
a fortune teller. Homed.
The cure for ennui:
Cornell's shadow boxes.
Family of objects. His visitors
infrequent. Ballerinas came by
to drop off their shadows.
Silver trees, enchanting,
echo long legs in white tights.

At first the afternoon is a young man
going on about his tattoos and piercings.
But then a yellow jacket
claws the crisp flesh of an apple.
Beauty and decay, always passengers
on the same train.

LET'S NOT PRETEND

As the tundra thaws, the woolly rhinoceros
surfaces. Mud-caked carcass meets January.
We are hairy and we are coming up for air.

The sequencing of the genome.
Your hands are bits of stars.
If we out-speed light
we watch leathery legs
walk the cold mammoth steppe.

The unthawed specimen appears matted
and I draw it above the toilet with a mouth full of greens.
Bison and horses paw the snow

to reveal the grasses. May your spawn
not run out of air or water. I'm pressing
my face into this beast's thick rank hair.

BLOCK CAPTAIN

When we lived on Othello
our neighbors were mostly retired
with ceiling-to-floor
salmon-colored drapes.

Bruce from Oklahoma
wanted a woman to cook for him.
He wore bright white socks
and dress shirts with jeans.

It was no surprise
when an animal shit on his porch.
He once got angry
when I said something smelled like ass.

Maybe we needed to halt all conversation
and utter facts.
We are water.
The forests are burning over yonder.
They pulled down the horse statue with its rider.

SOMETIMES

we would visit pet stores in New York City.
In a room resembling a long closet
cages stacked and crowded
a green parrot stepped along his perch
toward a foggy mirror and back toward
dirty water. Finches were his neighbors
and their fine rose legs clung to the wires.
A branch of millet devoured.

One summer one of my lovebirds killed the other.
There are those that don't feel loved
unless they're smothered. Someone
tried to love you but you kept
canceling plans. I'm carving soap
into various animals. This one
is a prairie dog. It can't stop eating
and still its teeth grow too long. Like gates
that keep you from your reaching your cake.

BRINE

When you inhabit temptation
the ground, walls, and sky
soothe you with their song.
The ache doubles its efforts
and you smoke it out. Morning
lifts the scrim. I drop your bags off
at the bookstore where you'll limp in eventually.
Shampoo, an avocado, cologne.
It's half a day and four phone calls
to plan a way out of town.
Mice move in to the boarded-up cabin
and eat the sugar. They die inside the stove—
burning hair and bones. The trees agree
that everything is temporary. I dictate
a letter to a bigger sea. Float in the brine
of the afternoon.

IN YOUR ABSENCE

A rosy-headed centipede
glides from rock to rock.
To vanish isn't hard, you know.
The forest creaks as branch rubs branch.
Somewhere water carves a canyon.
The city, an able distraction from the self.
But here absence hides in everything.
A shadow is a ghost is sand settling
after a fight at the bottom of the sea.
I've set aside pieces of myself for a rainy day.
In this pillow case: a piece of nose, two toes,
a hunk of my left thigh.
A stick is a shovel without a head,
which makes fast work
of a partial burial
to be attended by the birds
and the centipedes who stir
beneath my feet. It's almost night, you know.

DRY LAND

I.
On Thursday he said
it had been twelve days.
He wandered into the bedroom
and put a suitcase on the bed.
I hear, I'll sleep in the park.
I'm not sleeping in this bed
where you slept with other men.
One of our black cats
licks a paw. Swipes it
over her face as if
she's in a soap commercial.
Young people talk so loudly
as they walk past outside. Like they
own the world.

Good morning, you say
staring at the ceiling.
It wakes me. You seem stiff
and pull the covers. You say
I use the comforter as a fortress.
It's been thirteen days.

Did you know the ocean
froze and people walked
to Chebeague Island?

To sit on an ice floe
with the creaks
of ice crowding out ice.

To be a bird collecting spider webs.
Weaving a bowl. There's a
line, an edge, a knife, a gray whale
came up to the boat in Banderas Bay.
Afterward your cancer vanished.
Can something vanish
that never existed?

II.
In July, the Fremont Abbey
basement is sweltering.
We drink our wine from plastic cups.
My dripping back leans against
the stone foundation. Storytellers
take the stage. Afterward
you show me your place
and we make out. You play
the drums in a band.
The landlord's dogs
crash around upstairs. You're talking about
New Jersey. How your dad delivered mail
and your mom would stand smoking
at the window. The neighbors used leaves
from nearby trees to fold meals into
and gift them. You danced
to keep your parents from fighting.
Dishes hit the wall and your mom fell down.
You put a record on and danced.

POEM ABOUT THE NIGHT

Outside the brick apartments, night
closes around its pearl. Witch hazel is busy
warding off snakes.

I don't think of you except in silence.
Shadow on shadow, the dark between branches.
Shirtless youth relieve themselves behind a hedge and throw cans
in a fountain.

Do not call the night plain. Hiss of green leaves
then the horn of the ferry leaving downtown. Hobos
smoke under pine boughs in the park. Pillbugs
carry their eggs in a pouch from house to house

where only night exists. It
doesn't care about your desires.
Rotting log and centipedes.
I slither under ferns.

SEATTLE, 2019

Afterwards, a younger man
would come by to finish off
the birthday booze from the party
with all of the ancient fifty-year-olds.
We'd pull on our clothes.
He'd walk home. I hope
he swerved into Dick's
and the salt and fat
ringed his mouth.
Preserved his lips
for another.

If you and I had met back then
before the place on Holly Street
before the dogwood
a red blaze succumbed
to green. Before the rabbits
swam across the sound.
It is their island now.

WE TALK

On Sundays I hear about the red squirrels sipping sap
from thawing maples.
When they invade the attic, the stuffing is pillaged
from the arms of a doll whose wind-up dog falls from a shelf
its metal legs rowing the air then still.
You stir beef stew under the attic, below thick slabs of snow
while the people seated in orderly rows fly high overhead
on their way to London to see Big Ben.
You say there's a show about a survivalist who sews his clothes
from deerskin in the Oregon woods. He eats huckleberries and lives
in a log. You say your neighbors are shooting a rifle. You hear that? The
line is silent except you are breathing.

BIRCHES

From the back of the cab
flipbook of trees and highway signs.
Then the dirt roads shaking the car loose.
A horse's breath when it lifts its head
and the aluminum mailboxes on tilted stems.
Everywhere bare branches as I near the house.

The gray pond beneath the heavens
holds swans whose tail-like necks
swing round to scan the verge for foxes.
Then plunge their heads into the bank
for roots, for beetles,
the greens that dangle from a dinosaur's jaws.

We turn into the driveway greeted by the old cape
with its thin and wavy windows, you're still here—
limping through the field toward the pond
to gather shoots for cat tail soup.

GENIUS

Twice you went back—
stood on the lawn
stared at the house
when the owners weren't home.
Beside you the ghost of the sheepdog
with all of its longing. Beside him, a cicada
screeching at the sun.
A young girl comes around the corner.
Stands at a distance.
Are there still chickens out back, you ask?
They rotted in the freezer.
The cat pulled the plug. That's right.
And what happened to Rex, the manx?
He got carried off by an eagle.
What about the father and mother?
She moved out ages ago. He died in the house.
And then what? We strapped all our sins
to a goat and pushed it out to sea.
How convenient. And now?
Everyone's happy. No one ever fights.

MATCHBOX

Instead of attending your party
I admire the red crossed back of a black box elder bug
overwintering in my kitchen.
Sucking mouthparts. Pierced the sap is drawn.
The box elder tree, full of sugar
is what she must long for.
Bug on bug on dangling seeds.
There's a cardboard room
that I made her. With a toothpick bed,
and a window with a picture of a box elder maple.
I hope she finds it comfortable in there.
I go to great lengths not to scare her.

TIRE SWING

The way I saw it
once you figured out the pattern
you could measure a particular
man. And the next man you met

even if he lived faraway in Atlanta
would zero out the first
so there was no risk.
Not a lick. A bone
found in a hedge after a storm
didn't cause much alarm.

These entanglements
spooky until with the side of a pencil
the outline of a thing shaded in
I measure the doubt again.

UNTITLED

Were a kinkajou to wrap its tail
around my neck to signal stern authority,
I'd wander the woods with it attached
in search of figs for it to cradle
finding the meat with its tongue.
I arbor. We intersect across the bed
and I peel an orange. Babies cry
outside in the rain. You sleep
in a hollow. Leaves rattle all around.

LOSING

It's still open, you know
but even 5 years ago there sat
the bookseller, shoe guy,
and museum security guard.
Mostly old men at the bar.

And here's a punchline:
one is dead, one is sober,
and the other still draws
everyday faces that stare
through you to ask,

what have you seen in this life?
At a poetry reading
the bookseller fell into
a pedestal and broke his teeth.

We all fall
and how final
down is on the ground. It's
as though no one can picture
that we once stood.

It's not entirely your fault
that you lack imagination.
I sought nights in the bookstore

with the frog ashtray and microwave
burritos. The slalom home

through hotdog steam at Pine & 11th.
Hugo House with its ghosts.
After I moved away everything smelled
like skunk, which smells like coffee
when it's faint. The wilderness can resemble

blood on concrete. He returned to find his teeth.
Once I baked a bird so golden
it became a church.
Once I baked a bird so golden
it became a church.

CHICKEN BASKET

after Solmaz Sharif

The eels must keep swimming.
Perhaps they CHEAT
pushed by the currents? Who resides
in estuaries with sturgeons
who are world weary? EELS.

I mostly recall the hotel carpet
with the beige serpentine PATTERN
carving the navy. Who is doing the carving?
As I get fatter I switch out boyfriends so that
each one accepts what beauty is LEFT.

One time you tripped on the shower curtain
and fell out of the tub. Then we FORGED
a new animal—quiet and shy. Alone I entered
the elevator. The chicken basket
came with fries. Ample, not DRY.

The waves want to push you down
drag you under. You are CRUMPLED.
The spider in the sink drowned itself it seems.
If you want to love, you must
wade through bad waters. Everything's a TEST.

LETTER TO THE OWNER OF AN OLD WOOL SUIT

The smoke from northern fires remained,
rats spilled into the walks of the park, and
your bird came back. I kept the window open
so it wouldn't go away. Calypte. Tiny visitor
what did you have to tell me?

Then room-to-room like a solitary fish
exploring the cabin of a sunken ship
and I the figurine saw it fly down the hall
entering my bedroom. Voices
of the triplets on an outing to the park

sliced through Sunday's calm.
With a scowl I slammed the window shut.
The bird would turn up.
A tuba-like horn sounded the departure
of the afternoon. The hummingbird clung

to an old wool suit in my bedroom closet.
A shiny green brooch with a red capped head,
which I gently clasped and unhooked.
Carried it into the hall
into piercing late day sun,
which caused the bird to glow.

ACKNOWLEDGMENTS

"Birches" was first published in the San Pedro River Review, Vol. 9 No. 1, Spring 2017.

ABOUT THE MAINE WRITERS & PUBLISHERS ALLIANCE

Founded in 1975 by a group of small presses and writers, Maine Writers & Publishers Alliance (MWPA) has worked for decades to enrich the literary life and culture of Maine. We bring together Maine writers, editors, publishers, booksellers, and literary professionals at all stages of their careers to sharpen craft, create community, and celebrate great writing. MWPA has an active, growing membership of more than 1,500 literary professionals from all sixteen counties of the state and beyond. In 2021, the MWPA held ninety-five writing conferences, workshops, and events in locations across Maine and online. To help make our programs accessible, MWPA offered nearly $30,000 in scholarships and fellowships to Maine writers at all stages of their careers last year.

ABOUT THE MAINE CHAPBOOK SERIES

Between 1983 and 1999, thirteen chapbooks were published by the Maine Arts Commission in collaboration with a series of small Maine presses, and then by the Maine Writers & Publishers Alliance, as part of the Maine Chapbook Series. Each year, a nationally known writer served as the judge and selected a manuscript for publication. In 2019, the MWPA re-started this beloved series.

PREVIOUS MAINE CHAPBOOK SERIES WINNERS

Ruth Mendelson, *Sixteen Pastorals*
Theodore Press, 1983
Selected by Philip Booth

Rebecca Cummings, *Kaisa Kilponen*
Coyote Love Press, 1986
Selected by George Garrett

Robert Chute, *Samuel Sails for Home*
Coyote Love Press
Selected by Charles Simic

Christopher Fahy, *One Day in the Short Happy Life of Anna Banana*
Coastwise Press, 1988
Selected by Mary McCarthy

Kenneth Rosen, *The Hebrew Lion*
Ascensius Press, 1989
Selected by Amy Clampitt

Denis Ledoux, *Mountain Dance*
Coastwise Press, 1990
Selected by Elizabeth Hardwick

Besty Sholl, *Pick a Card*
Coyote/Bark Publications, 1991
Selected by Donald Hall

John A.S. Rogers, *The Elephant on the Tracks and Other Stories*
Muse Press, 1994
Selected by David Huddle

Candice Stover, *Holding Patterns*
Muse Press, 1994
Selected by Mary Oliver

Sis Deans, *Decisions and Other Stories*
Maine Writers & Publishers Alliance, 1995
Selected by Cathie Pelletier

Peter Harris, *Blue Hallelujahs*
Maine Writers & Publishers Alliance, 1996
Selected by Roland Flint

Rhea Cote Robbins, *Wednesday's Child*
Maine Writers & Publishers Alliance, 1997
Selected by Sven Birkerts

Ellen Bryan Obed, *A Letter from the Snow*
Maine Author's Publishing, 1999
Selected by Lois Lowry

Suzanne Langlois, *Bright Glint Gone*
Maine Writers & Publishers Alliance, 2020
Selected by Martha Collins

Brandon Dudley, *Hazards of Nature*
Maine Writers & Publishers Alliance, 2021
Selected by Sigrid Nunez

Coco McCracken, *The Rabbit*
Maine Writers & Publishers Alliance, 2022
Selected by Melissa Febos

ABOUT THE AUTHOR

At the beginning of the pandemic Sasha Goodwin moved back to Maine after thirty mostly good years in Seattle. She grew up in Pownal, and lives in Auburn now, with two black cats and a young pit mix named, Cheddar. In 2017, she completed an MFA in Creative Writing through the Pacific University low-residency program in Oregon.

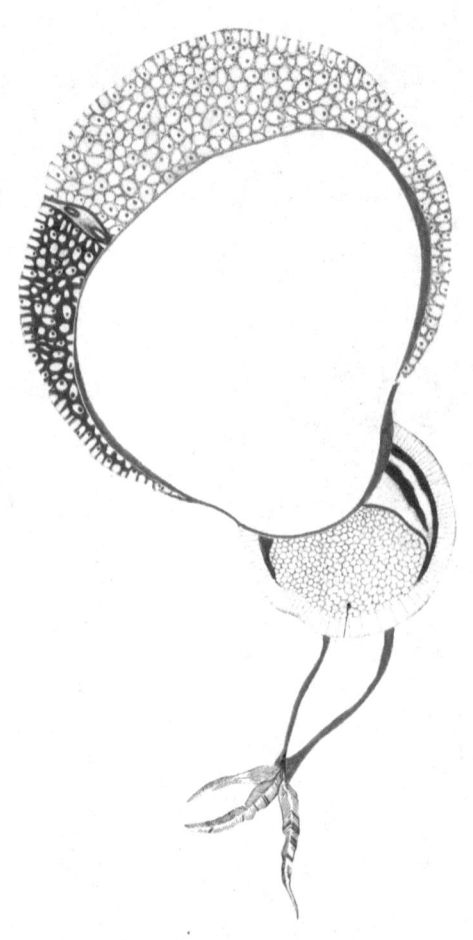

www.ingramcontent.com/pod-product-compliance
Lightning Source LLC
Chambersburg PA
CBHW010004110526
44587CB00024BA/4018